by Robert Kelly

Armed Descent
"The Exchanges"
Her Body Against Time
Round Dances
Enstasy
Lunes
Lectiones
Words In Service
Weeks
The Scorpions
Song XXIV
Devotions
Twenty Poems
Axon Dendron Tree
Crooked Bridge Love Society
A Joining
Alpha
Finding the Measure
Sonnets
Statement
Songs I-XXX
The Common Shore
A California Journal
Kali Yuga
Cities
In Time
Flesh Dream Book
Ralegh
The Pastorals
Reading Her Notes
The Tears of Edmund Burke
The Mill of Particulars
The Loom

Editor

A Controversy of Poets

THE MILL OF PARTICULARS

Robert Kelly

Black Sparrow Press – Santa Barbara – 1977

LIBRARY OF CONGRESS CATALOGING IN PUBLICATION DATA

Kelly, Robert, 1935—
    The mill of particulars.

    Poems.
    I. Title.
PS3521.E4322M5   811'.5'4   73-15571
ISBN 0-87685-173-1 (cloth)
ISBN 0-87685-172-3 (pbk.)

Some of these poems first appeared in magazines: *Antioch Review* (the Festschrift for Mr Gordon Cairnie), *Caterpillar* (Clayton Eshleman), *Hearse* (E. V. Griffith), *Ikon* (Rob Harmon, Harold McGee, Jonathan Post), *Intrepid* (Allen de Loach), *New Work* (John Weber) *Open Reading* (David Bromige), *Red Crow* (Thorpe Feidt), *Tansy* (John Mortiz), *Tree* (David Meltzer), *Sulphur* (RK).

Ralegh was first published in a limited edition printed by Saul and Lillian Marks at the Plantin Press for the Black Sparrow Press. "Aithers" and "A Praise of Ornament" first appeared as broadsides, printed by Helen in Annandale.

Second Printing

to Helen

CONTENTS

prefix:) Against the Code 11

Chambers 12
Llanto for Steve Jonas 13
Elgar's Second Symphony 16
Occulation of the Sun 18
The crowned man 19
Juncture 20
For Charles Olson, a six-months-mind 21
The Sound 23
In Mahler's Sleep 25
Ralegh 27
Linguistics 29
Feasts 32
The Search 35
Then we came out & saw the moon 38
The Customs Inspector 39
A Fragment for Stravinsky 41
Eve of St Mark's 42
A Red-Figured Cup of the Onesimos Painter 43
Jungle 44
The Centerfielder 45
Golden Gate 46
The Siege 48
Love Song 1 51
Love Song 2 52
Dakota 53

A Book of Building 57

Of these Heroes proposed 85
Morning Hymn 86
The Flowers of California 87
Coming 91
February's Last Song & Dance 92
A Romantic Revival 93
The Mill 96
Equinox 1972: The Surfaces of Spring 98
The Leaves 100
A Measure 102
Three Tunes 103
The Antiquarian 104
Two Love Stories better than average 105
The Return 106
Summertime 107
Waiting for the Barbarians 108
NY 97 109
Aithers 110
A Praise of Ornament 111
Orion's Cave 112

The Van Eyck workings:
Arnolfini's Wedding 119
The World 127

Notes 163

THE MILL OF PARTICULARS

AGAINST THE CODE

Language is the only genetics.

Field
"in which a man is understood & understands"
& becomes
what he thinks,
becomes what he says
following the argument.

"When it is written that Hermes or Thoth invented language, it is meant that language is itself the psychopomp, who leads the Individuality out of Eternity into the conditioned world of Time, a world that language makes by discussing it."

So the hasty road
& path of arrow
must lead up
from language again

               & in language the work be done,
work of light,
          beyond.

"Through manipulation and derangement of ordinary language (*parole*), the conditioned world is changed, weakened in its associative links, its power to hold an unconscious world-view (consensus) together. Eternity, which is always there, looms beyond the grid of speech."

11

CHAMBERS

Tested along the slope the bee walks, down
into the flower
    where the sweet release takes
place without murder

     a regularity
over the flowering field
       even the likelihood
of a number, a simple number
         laying itself
against the cheeks of things
         to make a count

probabilistic, peaks smoothed out,
         degraded
recencies on a smitten planet.

        These link
one after another to dream, convoy
of them steadily shunted,
      salt lake
& never an ocean,
      charity & new belief.

As follows:
     that there be a pattern
made up of as it were innocent flowers
in innocent repetition
      and the whole
texture thick in the mind & not
making men mad, me mad
      & not at night, open,
where the bee's convention
is not sinister, does not imply
a desert of will nearby
      across which
all the light
all the light
    has to bend to reach me

then I would go down & understand that earth.

LLANTO FOR STEVE JONAS

New voice.
And the old
basalt
comes back from the moon

search for porphyrins,
records of organic life

so that we billion our way beyond the earth
in search of our own lost powers

went to the moon
to have contact with our dead

who speak to us from ancient rocks,
no ferric iron, much titanium

cut off from quarrelsome Oberon. We are
our dead, & listen to the discarded voice.

*

Then the poem also
is a hum from the dead
to which we living
bring stops & spirants,
mouthing with our soft
perishable lips,
sonants in our bones.

Graves told us that every poem was about the moon.
Alchemy is Jehovah. Every poem
is a message from the dead to the living.
Love you. Cut off from women
the Hermit wanders his own urethra, chopping
wood for the fire. No moon. The dead & the dead.

*

If there were a place of danger we would find him there,
hypochondriac the better to be at the mercy of it.

Let the dust of the place be the red powder,
find death in the unlikeliest places, the chance
is the only chance we have. The fact of death

simplifies the message (as even the stupidest
magazines give evidence),
                        the fact of death,
gradus ad Parnassum, his meter finally
understood.

*

Death is the grade of Magus,
9 circles equal 2 squares
equals 6 feet under & his Word declared.

Pass in & out of incarnation.
The Magus declares his Word
& the world comforts itself
supposing it has understood.

*

He knew about money,
where it came from,
how it killed Kennedy,

how the Ace of Pentacles
contains in its disk
one central point

which by von Staudt's geometry
outside the circle
becomes infinitely big.

The point taken out of the circle
becomes the world. It escapes
definition. It killed him.

*

He was black but could
pass for silence.

To mourn him,
one silent cat.

The ocean
does not move to a new address.

On Beacon Hill
a policeman looks at the moon.

ELGAR'S SECOND SYMPHONY

for Jonathan Williams

A patchwork quilt
in old countries,

shame for a man
to have no religion.

The lime tree?
                    Morning
over the hill
when grey
is a primary color?

Repeat the way the sparrow does,
variation & dance, nothing big.

Patchwork—
homespun is fashionable
if you can get it.
They drive out here
on the Lord's day,
we bong the chapel bell
to make them think god.

*

Winter apples of Annandale
lie back of the road,
                    deer
chewed them, snow quilted them over,
now snow leaves them alone.
Spring starts this month
all over again.

*

Even in these fields
I walked with him.
Night fell.

All the owls
understood the thermometer.

Theater of a critical surgery,
this quarter-acre
the last footstep in Eden.

*

This music moves me more than I can say.
If I were suspicious I'd think about that.

But it *is* here, & what I hear
is beautiful. I go along with it

trusting, its big soft floppy heart
companionable, traveling.

                            Freedom
just past that locust tree.

*

Edom. When it sounded like this
all the time. When the vicar
still wore horns & the choros
of naked girls circled
widdershins around the church,

circled around me & I
married every one of them, every one,

& a voice from the earth cried out
I love you, my son, my last born.

OCCULTATION OF THE SUN

total over Atlantic, south & Mexique.

After two thousand years, earth moon & sun line up
to rime with the eclipse when Jesus died

(two nights ago, *Très Riches Heures*
crucifixion in the solid light of eclipse,

soot & ash from Enkidu's otherworld,

Christ dies on the cross.

And now this eclipse
ends the public cycle of Christian time,
Christ underground, the hidden Imam,
daimon,

Atlantis come to light & our Christ
becomes us in the dark

(we go into the dark
to take all the words
back from the public trivial light
& cache them again in us

seed

flower time past,

the bright hard seed
cast again anew
into our dark earth.

And now the balsamic moon
hurries on its way
to close the gates of earth
& dark the seed

end of summer in the world
& we begin

the crucifixion's finally done.

THE CROWNED MAN

The crowned man & red-fibred heart
overlooks the docks. Here, if anywhere,
the alien vision rides on the water
& reads itself into us (as Dante slips into the moon)
cleaving nothing, separating no two
lovers, but being heard in the dense
everything there is.

                The crowned man
is coated with sweet oil, his buttocks
slip pleasantly each against other,
he makes no noise. Mostly
he is taken by his eye & very common sense
& then he is led prisoner,
they braid blue flowers, early ones of spring,
into the fibers of his heart & then
what a fool he is.

              He has seen that broad
dappled water, surface of the mind
always informed & never informed
& they cant take him away from it or it from him.
The oil smells sweet as he passes by
between the angers & ardors of uneasy peace
past pale houses that dont watch the news
& buses filled with small captured animals
being transported to an empty book.

JUNCTURE

the highway that feeds
onto the Hollywood Freeway
is itself fed
(everything moving from right to left)
by an even more crowded street

where it all comes together
a square yard of cinders
from which
stands up a vigorous palm

I will believe in this,

power of life to balance

even in Jefferson's America
whipped to its knees
by the self-defeating
local powers
he allowed to men
who crave the light too little
& the dense
comforts of mortality too much.

Jeff stares out from the penny stamp
like a man watching hailstones flatten his corn—

I give him this palm tree

trusting at last in the earth
to injure & restore.

FOR CHARLES OLSON, A SIX-MONTHS-MIND

following the day
over the smokestack of the hospital
day gone down behind
       "may indicate the existence
of a neural mechanism which conveys the information
'in back of' "
      following a dead man to make
sense of the way he moved
         (loved)

& we are masters now or
I am master, the days
belong to nobody else
& the colors of the world

spell out their only word.
Attend, that the edge
stay hard, brave
as an idiot, a woodpecker

in the whole forest, stanza
of gluttony, every
surface must be probed.
A locomotive

could go through this
door I'm talking about
where a man
vanished & a city
predictably remained & girls

who should know better hate
subways & the noise of getting there.
Reverent attention
is not a matter alone of flowers

though flowers are so reliable
(the rose I cut you
in a romantic dream that hot
night last night just

before dusk, smashed
to the floor when the truck jerked,
that scentless, stolen
now ruined rose, dropping
petals & my fingers trying
not to thorn only
made it worse, that rose
darker now, stepped on,
now on the house-floor, a whole
fucked up rose

told
in its dangerous fragility
squashed flat, dark red,
bloodstain it so easily
came to resemble, I am attentive
to it now it's dead,

not a matter of roses only
but of all things
easy or not easy to kill
that do contrive to mean

something before the day goes,
harbor silts up, fish
rot in the dead lake & the
fire of time has its way with us)

the door
was the matter of his gesture
the kind of druid rock
that points to sunrise, tells
us all night long
where that's got to be,

natural image
or metaphor, bridge
halfway to morning,
dangerous as any
beautiful unfinished thing,

legend of getting there,
follow the dry white
bones that show the way,
all the dead flowers.

22

THE SOUND

First she heard a sound
like thunder,
bright sky

or heavy armchairs
moved
on the floor above her

when she was alone in the house
so she went out
when the sun

came through mist
& walked into the shadow
of a maple on the soft road

she heard far off
a hammer in the woods
she followed it

down along the stream
to the second waterfall
there was a man

"I am building" he said
& went on hammering,
she watched the pale

groaning wood, his arm
swung from the elbow
going down

"I am the human soul"
she said
"& I heard your hammer

in my only woods"
"I am building" he said
"a house or a table,

a horse or a child,
springtime & little
flies with golden wings,

you hear the sound
of thunder from an
empty sky"

"I am an actress
in this play" she said
& there was the

thunder again
though his hands were
still now, his eyes

fixed on her,
wondering.
"I suppose

you are no one
& this hour
betrays me

now I am near
the end of my work.
Go back home

& let me settle
this strife I have
with the old wood,

the seasoned wood"
she heard him
but the thunder

was all over her mind.

IN MAHLER'S SLEEP

an archaic austerity
comes out of the ground

(bird skeleton, snake skeleton,
no redundancy)

comes out & confronts the sea.

*

& even the Cycladic vastnesses
were tricked to stand
                              unlimed,
the big rocks cut true
hang true;
                    courses of specific gravity,
each rock remembers
the kernel at the center of the earth,

is loyal to that energy. Affinity.

*

The sack that holds the sandman's sleep
is stitched of many birds, feathers still on,
beaks still on & they cry out,
                              source of the high-frequency terror
our throats try to imitate
at the gates of nightmare,
                              groan of ancient door
we struggle to keep closed.
                              Wake dry. Larynx tight.
Our waking
is the last articulation of the dream.

*

In Mahler's sleep the yellow houses
fill with wise peasants, dead sheep
hang near the ovens, summer evening
is coming, air pale, the picture

25

precise as a glass of wine.
                    Mice
wait outside the granary
for a saint's permission to enter & eat
                    —their whole lives this tiny hunger
never stops.

A rabbi with a hardon
teaches the whole world,
bellows from his window
an ancient cockcrow
he learned from the heart of night.

                    *

By the stream almost dark now
the water lilies he thought they were
turn into a woman in green silk
who sits in the shallow water.
When he sees the sunset through her
he knows he's been tricked again,

once again his only friend is far away
travelling the emperor's road, dust, blue
distance, his only friend is
far away, he wakes with the distance in mind,
it stretches out, a definite number of
some measure, he's forgotten the number
& only brings to mind the direction:
                    the way the shadows point,
towards sunrise.

                    *

But morning is a crystal & a crystal is a stone.
A man lives three times longer than a hawk
but a bird can lead the man to the stone.

Trapped by the morning sky
the hawk falls out of his dream.

The austere thing is warm in his hand.

RALEGH

Caught in the window
breath of air
   lately on the big round wood table
 under the spruce, a level
outside to work on
   & let the air love me.
 The children of light
  summon this apparition,
church in the world . church of the world,
angel disguised as a spruce tree)

  *

    Ralegh appears in the dusk,
his queen a lost memory:
    "I was kinder when I loved her
& sailed to the island for her,
    this spindle island
half as big as the world.

   Tell her for me
  the years delight to pass
  & the cool air of July
 is sweet under love's trees.

On this big roll of parchment a map of these fields,
    thousands of miles, waters,

& on the little vellum folded in four
  my plan of the City
 we will one day begin to build her—

    the legend is in cipher
   to protect our studied proportions
  from foreign architects. .

     The stone she sent me
  casts no shadow.
    Tell her for me
   in love's name
   we will go

on trying forever,
rising & falling on the sweet
wave of the
work she gave us.

Quincunx in the garden, a knot of simples
round me as I write, I smell them around me
all afternoon as I thank her for my death

& all the Last Things,
                         tansy, campion, rue, basil,
          stavesacre,
their air blows kindly through my house

where in the evening fire I see the faces
of all her lovers
dancing with her, amiable, not too fast,

& therein even her particularity
merges in all
lovers whatsoever

in that glowing white hot place
                         below the flame
in the heart of the incandescent wood
where all the images stand still."

LINGUISTICS

1.

That stirs the way of seeing it,
vocabulary
of a poor people
                    rich in iliads,
in things & defined acts

                        perceptions of use
in the brief daylight.

Any sane man hates the cold & dark.

Mihrab.   Turn this way
(away from what you are)
pray
outside your geography.
                    The clock
will never be invented.

2.

Language of a besieged minority,
our words & theirs.

                    To build a house
            first paint the door
blue, wall white. A box
of song birds at every door.

Greek islands. So when the killers
come to kill
you have a simple word to say
known only by those about to die.

The great secret
but you leave it to the singing birds to say.

3.

When the set is properly grounded
your receiver will pick up
light verse of the gods
& detailed instructions
sent hourly from the Great Bear.
Fang music of Mercury
is easy to get, & steady
sighs from the exasperated Moon.

The problem is Earth
& again, the problem is Earth.
Who would believe these messages
cracked on the tongue like sticks
across the knee,
                        say it & spoil it?

To hear it at all
implies the transmission is false,
property of the atmosphere to deceive.

4.

A change had happened
& a different language
poured through his throat—

"I'm home! *This*
is America, not that hot
banana continent
swarming with frightened men"

He had his hands together, loose,
& looked into the dark between them
where a little light came through
colored by his skin.
                        He watched
till stars came out
& gave them the names he loved
lifted off the map of the lost republic.

5.

Shining words so that they cream for you
& spill unexpected breakfasts—that's
a work for Petronius or Strato,
                                    some
wild-eyed overcultured lastling
born the wrong year to be a hero,
a sex-fiend with a prose style.

A knowledge of the future
is what the close
study of written texts provides,
given a reader
wise with natural sympathy:

in some book is recorded
each thing will ever happen.

That is not style.
These words now
are part of your future
(not just that I'll be there for breakfast)

& the least song
rimes with the end of the world.

FEASTS

festivals
are religion
a bland pain
can extend
or block energies
we
come together
we exchange
our dreams
for dinner

the diner
has come from his privacy
timid with foreknowledge
trying to be open
his balls
strangely glow & his heart sings
far away where the woman
he had imagined
survives even the
national food

like a lute
compelling wisdom
from a room he cant enter
he hears her
in the excitement of his blood
his heart quiets
around his certain lust
& the ill-assorted
revelers
appear at the table

that could be board
of education
so solemn, food-heavy,
cracking jokes
with the last flicker of life
gastric salutes
to the immediate
commodity

of all our values,
the Thing

itself,
cooked to a turn
bought out of life,
hearty
victim of fake heartiness
holds the center,
sexuality
changes hands,
a hand desires
& a fork lifts

& mouth
(among so many silent
such silence)
starts to take in
that should be giving,
swallows its own glow
stifles desire
like a thief hiding merchandise,
old dreams crack
& the nut rolls out

This is the whole world
two hemispheres
& memory of shell,
good aromatic taste
when the teeth meet
& farewell sun
of all our marriages
they are filled with hasty
meanings
they belch

a jag of nut
bites his tongue
feeble fight back
& he remembers his dream!
Love
led him to this house
where love was murdered

by bulk affection
for the sake of a grail
now a dirty dish littered with bones

he burns
to declare
his experience:
boy becomes man
man mounts
the cross of woman, shouts
in the middle of the world
then is sold, Joseph
into the dark pit
by all his brothers, dinners, relations

with greasy lips now at this table,
his wisdom
quiets with a corrupt
vast sympathy for all things
trapped, beginning to like the trap, he groans, bursts
free into the science of himself,
smashes the cup that stands for her
& now has to travel
alone with dying echoes of his sense
into the thick world outside may he find her again.

THE SEARCH

inside it
pieces of noise
a drum rolls
a head

rolls it was too
slow to
see them
the train gets in

to Harvard Square
final white walls
no travel
will work from here

we are blown
wide open, a story
or song
out of some woods

cracks open
starts to sing
our transgression
is mortal

sing or die
cries the fairy
prince or princess
no choice

but to rule
myself by song
take counsel of
hear

what launches
out of my mouth
from the train
we saw a river

that makes sense

red houses
a cold bandshell
winter island

I cant give you
any more
the theme of what I
was looking for

keeps coming back
find it did I
find it I didnt
can I still

go home
was it a book or
record, some contact
personal enough

god knows
but not good
enough, not the right
person

or the true time,
something
walks from the
station

in my defeat,
fancy food stores
last corner stand
of underwear pornography

can I surpass
this not naked
city, the fake
directness of streets,

what I was
looking for
recedes
towards the river

on a street
where there are only
houses
it cannot be here

what it was
was in crowds
in public
& lost there

lost everywhere
I could not chance
to be more specific
than it was

whatever it was
naked solitary
in its immense
particularity.

THEN WE CAME OUT & SAW THE MOON

not the moon

That woke me
& at the end of the hall
the moon five days past full
risen bright above the sallow air

deceived me over the trees,
had everything died while I slept?

A bad time to wake up
but it was time,
                dark spaceship under the moon
had sucked my thought
out past the orbit of Uranus
where Eros ends.

They left me a line & a half from a black Veda
to explain the motionless.
They left a moon in the sky
to explain itself.

                The touchstone
                fell
                under leaves
                it hid
                I would wake it
                call it
treat it with flint.
Because I have no children.
Because I face southwest
& the moon will cross my path.

        And what I want is three birds to cross the moon
on their flight to the everywhere stone.

THE CUSTOMS INSPECTOR

Everything starts in the same way.
The eye grows weary
of checking where they hide their diamonds.
These amateur smugglers
put them everywhere
but mostly in the same predictable places—
in vulva or anus
armpit, shoe (how can they walk?)
perineum behind scrotum
(how can they sit down?)
in their mouths so that they mumble
in their ears so I have to shout.

They're smuggling diamonds from the East
but most of them, maybe all,
have forgotten they're doing that
& mostly think of themselves as innocent—
it's been a long trip.
Where's the diamond? What's a diamond?
that's what they tell me
yet when I look at them quietly
my eyes not accusing, just being clear
on them & at them,
they get nervous, anxious, soon reveal
where they hid the stone

or where—without even their full
conscious awareness—the stone
was hidden in them by professionals
or for all they knew
maybe it hid itself in them.

I can tell by the way they squirm
what part of their bodies it's hidden in.
And then I have to call it out,
treat them carefully
& make them discover the stone themselves.
They feel better when they find it.

I'm not supposed to touch them
but sometimes their grace or awkwardness

touches me, & I move to help,
be of help, remind them of all the places,
dark hollows of themselves.
Sometimes I reach in & touch the stone.

A FRAGMENT FOR STRAVINSKY

[Hearing the Dumbarton Oaks Concerto in a week of death]

What is sex it is not a flower or a flower only
blossoming from belly not a tree with infinite hands
on everything it is a power & I do not meet it square
It makes the world go round it does not turn
it is fixed glance it flickers it burns & returns
abolishes both ends of itself it is all mouth
And in my dark I turn from it & the wasted season
it is the length of death inside me I have paid out
never finding end, all men delude themselves
there is a work they can finish, every coming
is an end to it but not its end.

EVE OF ST MARK'S

Tonight the dust's footprint shows the about to die,
wraiths at churchdoor

                    & what we always affirm
is more of the same.
             Maybe it is each name
we cling to that condemns us,

                    our track, our well-known
footstep in the ashes.

             The bitterest wine
is to be no one

                but it cleanses & heals.

A RED-FIGURED CUP OF THE ONESIMOS PAINTER

She cant be more than 19
& spreads her legs joyfully
to her skinny old lover,
he gestures
at her trim belly & wide open lap.

He is dark & looks
in bad shape. Behind his back
he hides a dildo
just in case—
she is so young & open, her almost smile
is so happy, more wonderful even
than her firm breasts & lifted thigh.

The old man comes on
in eager doubt
he is a satyr but his day is past.
It is St Paul
doubting his flesh
& all flesh with it
damned to imperfection.

But her eager smile
will not measure him,
it is not a performance, not a test,
she is open & he
is welcome.
Just let him get inside her
& there will be no death.

JUNGLE

The green that grows from me depletes my soil,
is not variety, does not mulch down
a complement of intimate support. Growth
stands between me & the sun, the branches
repeat endlessly the same ideas, the same form.
Rain comes through, I get the leach of it
colored by monotonous unstable leaves.
I thought these feelings into place & now
feelings have no place to think their own.
The tree trunk is will, skeleton of earlier design
that leaves no room for breath or search or care.
A jungle has no heart. The core of it is to be more.

THE CENTERFIELDER

At the brink
a lovely rain
          & light
where it's coming from

I hear a sequence
rhythm
of an exact unfolding

necessary
between people like us
when I so much am
in love with substance

catch it there
in the golden outfield
far from the batter's
creative wrists

I can do nothing unless it comes down.

GOLDEN GATE

1.

ripcord of the setting sun   n dwat
he passes, into the What is
in the underworld,
                    a landscape
          of specific information

through birth canals
into the dark,

                    this fat world our placenta dragged
(still ravenous ghosts)
                    after into else
Else is Egypt.
          Be careful when you land, the old
beanpoles tilt a danger,
                    beware the eyes. Seen
from the hills (cold at night, cold enough

for a breath), to restore.
                    That's not so smart,
that lets us deceive ourselves
into thinking it all begins again,

whereas it dont. I heard that language
once before, it welled
in my westernmost ear, I wallowed

& that was the end of me. Long this fall.
How lord. This space
varnished with air beneath thy Going Down.

2.

He is who he is in the underworld
the meatrack, the doorsill,
forgotten dialect.

3.

Give it a chance
it isnt as young as
who used to be,
        amid the fatassed syrian
hierodulai, who proffered
god's love
in all particulars

to the necessary stranger
determined
on such holiness.

        The central issue of this century
        is sanctity.

Pylon
of the Eleventh Hall.

Dwat. Where the sun goes at night
& we go with him,

        count the serpent forms, the bound men,
the men in desert armor
from the western coasts,
Garamantes, Hu Fasa, Rommel,
        as-sudan,
        do not go into the rock.

Give it a chance
to work inside you
south of bellybutton,
in the shadow
of our first local connection,
        mother friend, salt of all the syrtes,
oasis in the night of
where the sun goes out

past us, into the temple where the temple harlots
wait for him. Anoint him. Anneal his glass face
over the no-time fire & make him come again.

THE SIEGE

Evening & be wary—
the host of love
sits down before this city
minded to enslave

swerved the river
from its normal fall
& dammed it
where the uneasy light

dapples ten miles off
a scorn on bright days
when the Defender
stands on his walls

overcome by irony.
He sings:
Overcome & overdo;
The Lass that

Limed a Sailor;
My Kingdom Come;
Old Black Shoe; Our
Father's Fee

in Faiths of Old.
Besiegers dont care
(if they cared, truly,
they'd go home)

they watch him &
notch the fitful
arrow now & then.
They know while he sings

nothing much will happen.
His troops are mutinous
(they know) but lazy.
Their day will come.

Meantime he hums,
that part of Mahler
where the oboe cries
because the hills

stretch out so long
& everything is far away.
He cries a lot himself,
the warriors

have some sympathy
as little as they like his
huff & puff. They could,
after all, hit him,

drag him down with grapples,
outshout him in their
shrill contralto
(early trained to war).

Not by chance
the menstruating soldiers
pitched their tents
closest to his walls

they wash their blood off
while he's overhead,
they hang white cloths
& blue ribbons,

they smile up at him.
It's been a week
since he's eaten,
his troops have food

he's even too proud
to rule his servants
—let them learn
by themselves to serve

is what he thinks.
That's why Love's so

sure she's cornered him.
He will lose

& the great bronze
gateway open.
It will be silent then
& mostly

the neighborhood wind
will have its way.
He'll come out
leading his troops

feasting, he'll walk
past the Amazons
& stand bareheaded
at the green silk tent

waiting her turn.
She may come out
& he may recognize
a face like light

over the hasty dam
or clouds of midges
just before dark
or a face he knows

too well to recognize.

LOVE SONG 1

The grunion
are coming

it is complex
& predictable

they arrive
connected with the moon

              men
        who have lived longer
        run to capture

this subtle sort of thing that
doesnt happen every night. I'm

not interested. Everything I care for
happens all the time.

LOVE SONG 2

It's the way you walk
& if you dont like
that it's the way you
talk. Or any other

ordinary thing that
rimes with the ordinary sun.
This is my best deal:
yourself exactly as you are

or anything at all the way it is.

DAKOTA

The sun took the top of my head off
& it was all in my head,
homoio-, homo-,
similar or same;
we couldnt get straight.

                        Sheepmen or cattlemen,
                   they all
                     left dust when they passed by
herding their preoccupations.
Whose side is mythology on?
                   It tells our time
we can fight it all our lives & never win.

Empty headed I turned my feet at last
to the country of energy along the road of being simple.

A BOOK OF BUILDING

A BOOK OF BUILDING

Cathedral

is of categories:
                    orders of architecture
I am here to employ) devise—

categories & fill them. The bright
personages (windows)
in an opaque life (Bruckner)

lifting the whole edifice
through Lust (ogive)
to the Limits of the Apparently Real,

the big white sky.

The proportions lie in tone, *not rhythm.* Interval, *not beat.*
Rhythm is didactic.

BIG BEN

big bell
of government
throng
of *demos*
swept under the shadow
the bell
casts

(the bell casts shadow into the ear, or,
sound is shadow

or
krateia is rule,
to have rule over.
They rule.

They are ruled.
It is the fate of any world
made of pronouns.
Pronouns arent people.
They do it,
they build the tower
& cast the bell
& ring it
till we go crazy
in what had been *my* night.
Demos, people,
us seen as them.

At least the tower points the right way.

The bell weighs tons.

(Bell-metal is complex alloy. The mixtures sound different.
Scales of alloy. How you sound. How I sound.)

Time to be born.

Some while after thinking about bells
I had a dream of breasts, big heavy ones.
That's an odd dream for me
since I am not
partial

but whole, the whole tower in the whole sky,
the whole woman
sounding

against a gunmetal sky.

Who is this woman
(it will be asked),
it is the woman without breasts
no vulva to distract
no head.
It is someone Less Luminous.
It is the Light's Own Shadow.

I see the sound of her
coming out where there should be clouds.

(*Interlude.* The Tool)

But the just what
I'm in is it

the old wood
handle of the
sticks out from
the newer metal
meant to re
inforce it I
like the old wood

garden trowel

under the

banana tree
its stalk looks
like a banana
surely, is it

a tree

not easily,

three

o'clock

one looks at the garden
freed
from ideas of the
garden all the

other ideas
weeds
not yet found
use for
aesthetics &

look, at,
the garden

but the just what
I'm in is it

old wood

a handle.

we are not responsible for horizontal mistakes
　　　　　　　　　　　　　　　—Luther.

THE LEANING TOWER

balances
our attention.
It eyecatches, it lures
persons to Pisa
who have no (presumably)
business being there.

Tons of concrete
keep it
from enlarging its act

(its 14
foot (top)
deviation
from the vertical.

A tower of a given height 14 feet off the vertical describes what
angle with the earth?
　　　　　　　　　On a certain day
　　　　　　　every year
　　　　　the leaning tower
　　　　　　　points off from Pisa
　　　　　　　　　at a certain star
　　　what star?

the finger pointing at the you-know-what.

The moon
is something else.
Nothing points to it
but american money
chinese fingers
yellow dogs coyotes
up the canyon

　　　　　　"you think that's the
　　　　　moon

62

                          up there
                  you're looking at?"

a lesson in spherical geometry.

All these stone buildings
make my teeth ache.

(*Interlude.* A couple of birds.)

Mountain Chickadee

". . . of our Western mountains
has a song of 3
high whistled notes.
He travels in little
groups among the conifers."

Gros Beak

olive patches closer
but first a big
strong blunt beak
tool, gear
to get meat out.
The grosbeak
constructs a universe
that makes use
of all his qualities.

This is true
teleology,
the world takes its form
as a consensus
of all the inhabitants'
image of their

"needs . . .
their capacities."

(What was the other bird?
The third,
a bird
out of a book:

the swallow.
Now through the bright rooms
the swallow
momently passes,

in one door & out the other,
a moment in light
between two darks.
King Ædwin's bird,

bird in the house.
Now this is human life
       & the swallow
           flits across the poem,

also a light room
between two conditions
better left dark

if only for the moment.
For the sake of the building
this is.

(stretto:)

        moment sake building is
          bird in house
             poem
          among thee)

Mountain chickadee (again)

      song of 3

      little

      among the conifers.

EIFFEL TOWER

Through the words
can be seen the high
blue sky.
          The building
is easy for birds

to penetrate.

The drawing I'm looking at makes the Tower seem to straddle the
Seine with its graceful art-nouveau flippers, two on each bank.
But it does not, though it were pleasant if it sometimes did, on one
of those summer midnights when nothing else is moving in the city.
Actually the Tower stands beside the river & you've never seen two
big close things pay so little attention to each other. Even Grant's
Tomb pretends to look down on the Hudson. But this Tower stands
there, unrelated to anything but the skyline & the ultimate womb
sky that obsesses it. And now, through a drawing, its poise plays
into my hands. How much rather would I study the groovy towers
of alchemy, the Buttery, la Sainte-Chapelle, or the north tower of
Notre-Dame I did even climb inside the damp stone, following the
turn of stairs as a man might read a horoscope, persuaded of cycles
& helixes. But I'm stuck with the Eiffel, neither old nor new, Antic
Technology rehearsing its stress formulas all day long & casting a
mile-long shadow in the afternoon. Reaches to what? Or even to
transform the lousy drawing into a three-dimensional model, like
those leaden Eiffel Towers tourists are supposed to bring home.
But the real lead is here in the bad drawing, the real lead is in the
name, Eiffel Tower, a name hard to hear without smiling, however
many neurotics may cast themselves from it. Lead. Lead. Or not so
neurotic. Turn gold in setting sun. Into that crucible, if it were licit
to proceed. Licit? Dull weary but full of promise, like a sentence
stared at too long, the Tower is distinct against the leaden sky.
Openwork, to encourage the seeds of gold.

I mean it's the easiest
building for birds.

I mean
is the signal
for variations,

66

I mean the easiest birds
can make sense of it easily.

It becomes what it had been
nostalgia, that plague
of cities

"if I didn't know better, I wouldnt be surprised"
Sneeze.

"The grey stripy cat" called *grisgris*
has vanished.
It is 4:32 p.m. in California,
the mountains play their
game with clouds
or the clouds
and so on.
Bruckner pulls out his watch
to check the time the last note is set down.
Ganz fertig. It is finished, per-
fected. Now he begins again
to work on it. Another year.
Another peek at the watch, *ganz
fertig* now, & still the work
continues, as long as breath lasts
the building goes on.

It is what I gladly see,
a mental building rising
through the sunlight of a
nice day. The tower
(Maison-Dieu) shattered by
lightning, prostrate,
gets to its feet again

leaving holes in it for birds to go through.

(*Interlude.* The Snail)

> Snail in garden
> unbelievable
> wonder of its house
> by "growth & form."

& here I wondered
how snails came in
when all the while they bear
a precise numeric architecture
out of time's mind.

By all the while I mean these thirty years
since I found a snail in our Brooklyn yard,
held on to it, tried to take
care of it, it ate its way
up the curtain, found two weeks later.
We unravelled the thread, it lived
& where was I, where was the end
of that story,

this new snail, this now snail
on a brown envelope where Helen put it,

a different garden, this,

> this is,

> this,
> & nothing else is.

Snail. Dodman. Carries his own house
& we have never gotten over that,

who cannot even sleep in what we are.

(*Interlude.* Some exposition)

Note 1

An anatomical drawing of a famous building.

Chest tones
from the corazón.

The building of a song
is long.

Note 2

Three notes, as of the chickadee;
or one note three times.
You cant have a song without three tones.
Note is a tone sideways or endways on.
A song is made of three.

I mean is made of thee.

Note 3

History of the French:

1803—Sale of Louisiana, & with it loss of a sense of west. Wheat.
1831—Première of *Robert the Devil.*
1859—Battle of Solferino.
1860—Verguin synthesizes a dye the color of battle. He calls it
        magenta.
1889—Alexandre Gustave Eiffel builds a tower.

The people who came before were *cathedrals.*
The people who came after were Artaud.

(*Interlude.* The Condition)

A house
is a piece of meat.

All over the neighborhood
dogs are howling, not barking, in a curious way.
They're not trying to communicate with men.
There is moan in what they do.
There are coyotes up the hill.

A house is meat but a building
is a tower, a fire, a word
spoken from the sky.
Birds fly through the words.

Under their wings the sky is secure.
Sure.

a keyhole
at the end of the street.
Though I saw it
I have little memory of the aperture
just what I saw through it

> (Long Beach, Long Island.
> Put in coins, two pennies,
> "What the Butler Saw,"
> extravagance of lingerie
> titillations flicked
> by in fast pages
> to suggest a motion
> picture
> like the Donald Duck
> book I had
> with no women in it.
> No pussy for Donald
> squawk squawk squawk.)

I call the arch a keyhole
but the door's bricked up.
Peel plaster, scruff of
white dust, neck, throat,
she was coughing, gasping
an hour later that very
cold night, tearing her
walls down, she could do it
why
          after so many years cant I?

(I got through the keyhole & saw)

(how scared that other, the first
Mildred was, Halloween, my father
rattled outside, hooted, ghosted
at the little window, she locked
herself in the bathroom
but even there didnt feel safe.
The Devil comes through keyholes,
I was the devil, I gibbered

71

at the keyhole, wiggled the key
to make her scared, ghost through
keyhole,

        poor kid from Carolina,
an islander, scared, hysterical
by the white man's All Hallows Eve
she taught me to believe,

                I walked
through the keyhole,
not Arch of Triumph, keyhole,
Rasputin, hole in ice, little
fat devil learning to forgive myself

(through the arch
into Washington Square
carrying Rilke towards the girls on the rim of the fountain,

that 14 year old expert, her skin so soft,
me 15 & looking older,
dumber than ever, I moved

(Grand Army Plaza, no one under the arch, an avenue away,
Ebbets Field south, Manhattan Bridge north, the apparent bound-
aries. But far away south Flatbush Avenue came to water, Marine
Park where Diane lived, where I grew up, learning my sister from
the ground we separately shared, grew up, Gerritsen Beach, Floyd
Bennett Field, lift of bridge over to Rockaway, Riis Park, the con-
fusions of Bay One, the Ocean I would cross to walk towards the
other arch

        & not go through.

Arches respect virgins. Built
by closed societies, late Roman,
French Empire, America after Gettysburg.
America Jay Gould. America Daniel Drew.
Money is endlessly virgin. The arch,
the blood spilt at Magenta, & always
in the shadows of the arches, tense
with merciless compassion, the anarchists.

(A Sermon)

There are now too many stories here. I catch the links of arches or notches, keyholes & ghosts. Now women enter, as they always do, that poignant shadow. But not a shadow. Woman is a primary, neither emanation nor spectre. Blake's tradition confuses Woman with Mother, & blames her energies for the ceaseless weaving on the generative looms. It is in her *place* that the shuttle moves, but it is in her power to make the shuttle bear a weft of light through the warp of her own energetic nature, yielding no child but light. The womb also teaches Emptiness.

woman *face*
head breasts
lion body wings
serpent tail.

The Egyptian is less feminine.
The intersexual face
is open under the nemyss—
it has nothing to hide,
has no secret.
It is a secret,
so can stare openly at the sun,
covered & revealed
by the purposeful
ages of sand.
Lion paws.

Alternative vision forces complex coordinates.
Wait & find a place.

                    (Bruno: "That's all I've ever
                              tried to find")
If the building works.

The Sphinx, obviously,
is a house turned inside out.

The paws define an avenue to her breast,
we slosh along it where the milk is running.

Galaxy we live in
between her paws
& all the rest

is mystery. Lion. Snake. Eagle. Woman
face & form,
the full breasts

an energetic milk.

A sphinx
is connection.

I rest between her paws
in something like peace.

A sphinx:
interpenetration of
physical body by
energy body

at least.
Sphincter.
Narrow pass.
Prose now
& rose later,
Steller's jay & chickadee
bird of paradise
blooming for Christmas
below the bananas,
the rock garden
I am supposed to tend.

The rock. The mist. The river. Ion swarm.
Four Elements
persuasive of our instruments.
The states of

       matter? A kangaroo.
Springbok. In dream the energy body
repossesses the world.

The poignant building
replaces my mind.

This is as far
as daylight syntax reaches.

Four & not three four
& not five four
& not more. Not more

than four.
Four & not
three & not
five,
        four & not more.

We dont get to Five
(till the dog comes home,
dog race movie game
the Dewey on Coney
Island Avenue, my ticket
was 5, a collie, the race
on the old old film
was run, was won
by Five, I won, all the kids
in the audience with Five
got what, a box
with a game in it, a spin
the arrow.
            Five was luck
& the collie
ran down the alley
alongside Mr Hoffman
limping back home
his lunch pail
lurching in big arcs
up & down

            leaving me
to find Five.
Quintessence.

The game is static,
locks in, my father,
Uncle Walter, Uncle Tommy,
Uncle Joe around the
walnut table, pinochle,
locked
        away from play,
I waited
for the air to clear,
waited for Five
            outside

the box, Five
will not fit in—
I used to think
that Five was Fire,
but fire
burnt Diana's house
& all her breasts,
Ptolemy's books, Luna
Park, the pier
in Hoboken
reaching for heaven.
Poem.
Or Five Is Poem,
news
from beyond
'the round earth's imagined corners'

outside the circle.
Yvan Goll: O pour
briser
un seul cercle!
or Five is Sleep,

& sleep
our firebrand,
Sphinx
wakes.
Fire Milk.
She makes her presence known
by joint,
          fuck of images first revealed,
Mars & Venus dangled in one net
with background of mosaic leaves,
holy marriage, opposites in bed,
she is lady
          (if she is lady)
of associations,
                    capable of magnetic parts, ultimate
building for its own sake.

(The Partiality of Sphinxes)

Her riddle
is resolution.

Connect,
reengage
in the detail of your whole life,

you are to find the pattern,
find you.

(The peril of conversing with sphinxes is didacticism.
Didacticism is to fall back on the authority of personal
history, accident of your opinions. Didacticism is
Marrying your mother.)

Only the simplest
syntax
betrays her
reveals her
copula
and.

(The Woman)

The woman
I thought
was face &
breast,

haunted
by those isolates
I painted her,
face, long hair
symmetrical down
over full breasts—

all by itself on the page
it looked like a cock & balls
(heavy breasts), those Roman
bronze playthings,

she spoke:

"That you
ultimate
a tree not
it is the least any
body for
you to come along"

What do I know of faces?
I heard the body speak
louder than personality
all my life, louder than faces.

(*Interlude.* The Faces.)

Face over dream.
The corridor is brain
I move
along it in mind.

It is an old story,
Bruno's magic house
keyed for retrieval,
my friend Arthur

hypnotized, walking
a hallway to a hooded
figure whose face he
would not look at,

screamed, would not
look at the book
held out for him, book
without words, the blank

caught his eye
& chained him
to know nothing, the glare
the beautiful

opaque light
from which we stumble
home, somewhere,
having no word to say.

Road
goes.
Tower & cube,
"A staircase
in one corner of room
in order to view
my work from another."
To make a picture
of the whole thing,
all the confusions
twang,
      the tower,
the dome, the arch,
the woman in whom
all are united
beyond identity.

Beyond me.
Not to be
anybody
locked
in that particular?
The noman's wine
I advertised
recurred in dream.
We were with another
couple, we danced
in a ring
on the beach.
The other girl was
smaller than you,
we danced awkward
very happy,
her breasts leapt,
her shirt was open,
I loosed
yours quickly
so you
would move as free,
round dance
beyond

any one,
the four of us
in our particular
sizes being
one dancing
by the sea.

1972

OF THESE HEROES PROPOSED

Clear gentle air
over Jesse James & male friendships
& womanless feats of the Heraclids

whereas the soft sky this morning
is bright just behind where some
flowers like peonies grow in shade

in the shade of a house.

Why dont they come in
who have played all night
at treason & its opposite

triumphs of pecking order & catastrophes of reason
gun bomb & bank
a woman only an
accomplishment
why dont you come in

*

The Heroic
silences itself in a bullet

the Hero
resembles a door

capable of extreme positions
without change of location.

*

I would were a flower
to which you might turn,
a woman in bed to you
in your anger.

A knock on the door & your
body doesnt mean anything anymore.

Things I get ready for &
                    MORNING HYMN

I can remember
hunting the landlord out last
day before eviction &
putting somehow money
into his hands
                    & phones still ring
announcing improbable conferences
in a world less
real day by day because
                    they're old in it & the young

schedule nothing. It happens
if it's supposed to
& at the right time.
                    Why do those men
lock themselves in time
where nothing ever happens & they wither?

Give them that thrust
where & whereby
ancient kingdoms
were made to
remember the sea

where all their loving came from,
veined marble & forms
they learned to find in it,
                    cut
it to stand in their houses
& be beautiful.

                    Sometimes it rained.
That rare Aegean rainlight
I call down now on the beauty of form

that it shine out of us, wet
intelligible & worth being loved

as we move, our skins at that hour
brighter than sky,
                    glistening with love's now or never.

86

THE FLOWERS OF CALIFORNIA
for George Quasha

Now the gate looks otherwise
& the Second Face
peers into time, smiles
with a dangerous smile
& calls his time

Acacia blossoms. The road
is yellow also down the hill
where the city
lies in light haze. The lies
of my austerity
correct themselves.
               It *is* out there,
is possible, no stance of renunciation
has to be taken. The Face
looks through the gate.

1 February, one fever
the words link to a beach
where women are walking
& the sea is boiling,
               a steam
of enterprise no one sits down.
Now this fever in the word
links back to the mornings
of human fear, when we began
to know what time had
in store for us, cuckolding us
who work to shape her.

And the fever began there,
heated up
          the beach . the boiling sea.

We went down there, carrying red berries of toyon and sprays of manzanita flowers heavy with a scent like jasmine, January, down under the waves to instruct that curious kingdom in the arts of fuck.
      Laurel crown, Umbellularia californica, headache leaves, vowed crown, wreathed with love and auspicious arrivals,

                                                                and
walked with the daughters of them there, the king, the queen,
along the white sandy bottom
                        Arisleus. To know the
                            sisterly, the woman
chosen by "blood"
                    is seawater, the genetic, the fake code.

"This instrument allows me. I have come back to you, as the yucca
promised when it fell. All these waves are chances of my dances,
heart on the head in the heart of your breath—all one, all mine to
be hoped, all mine."

(Daphne mezereum, spurge olive—corrosive to skin. The girl in
Russia, to choose a redness, put up with the pain to bring
                                                    color to
her life, her face eager, at the gate, waiting for her lover, to come
in.)

These leaves are friction.
                        (Friction's daughters.
                The whole family,
            Thatway & Friction,
                who begat
        Will & Want,
                    & their fair sisters
                            Permission & Suck,
by whom their father (furtively!) brooded
                        Thought & Memory, Mushroom & Mercy
whose in turn first child, crisscross bred,
                    was Wisdom herself,
                                who stole
                                the old man's eye!

And Wisdom had a daughter.)

Rhus vernix, poison tree, poison to whose flesh.
                            But Rhus ovata, sugarbush,
                        like tiny staghorn sumac,
                    also erect.
Pacific flora. Holy Wood.
                        (The canyon where she walked,
coming down from the acacia trees in bloom

her young breasts loose in the shirt.
She caught sight of me & shouted,
You've seen me before!)

There are only certain lines the hand runs along,
the song:
There is no play left in your fortune,
it all went west with the cookies.
No chance, no chance a tall
sequoia. Sempervirens, my lover's heart
speaks all night in Esperanto
to the girls on corners. Volapük?
You're the only cosmology I've got.

O Fortuna, mistress of each which
kosmos, lady, restore my fond belief
in your random fingers, o I need doubt.
The point of your pin is causality.
Plume. Feathers of tautology
bedeck your earnest overspinning head.
¡Yo no creo! It is west & forget it,
there is no music when there is no street.

(And that was our sweet encounter, our suicide supper, concluded
by fortune's cakes, which read as follows clockwise round the table:

"The street is responsible for its own perceptions.
Those who can do better had better.
This is America & we're all protestants together.
That is important to september.
Your only orders are March."

We left the handsome Manchu lady, moved past the enfilade of
dead poets, their lines whizzing out like arrows in a frontiersman's
nightmare. We reach at last the Barranca of Fertile Remorse,
inhabited by improbable indians. A goose honked by the mouth
of the culvert we crawl through to get in. Third from the sun.

Meadowlark.
My fortune was a magpie in Claremont I didnt see.
My arm cut bad, agave. Got
cut by the little greenhouse, view of the sea,
bayonet tree,

this distortion has a torsion of its own
I would be careful of you to remember.)

Quercus. Spiritus quercus glandi. Acorn medicine.
And the silk-floss tree
                        nubby
glistering yellow trunk,
                        a silk floss tree pointing towards Moab
or where the people wander,
                        a yellow wonder.
It turns out those berries are toyon.

*

Most pure spirit, let me wonder at everything all the days of our mutual life. To turn from wonders to wonders. To see the gorge or cleft in earth stand clear from the seductive embrocations of those girls at lakeside. Honey. Salt on whose? Yucca australis, thirty feet high, a tree to shadow in, the thought is thorn. Cinnamon or cassia, strips or chips? What they brew is a slave cup, I drink it down. Boca. Earth-mouth, vulva or cleft. With my pores wide open to gulp their juices in. Gulf or vacancy. Thought to be an island. Where she walks with all her kind. Their nakedness is hostility. California. Trichocereus, huge phallic cacti with swollen glandes move against the shadows of her coast to drink deep what is below her, to thrive on her most secret water, currents she forgot before she ever raised her angry arms to the sun. To go into her without belief & *still* be there!

COMING

The blue mouth of the shark
becomes the blue silk hung
canopy bed at Versailles,
a blue grinning cave, blue death Yama, Hevajra,
cave mouth

        a great blue harp
        strung with our lives

        (the first harp
was the great fish's jawbone,

        monster slain
into our history in the sign of music

*

or mouth of the blue shark
swims through the red
music of the bed

*

or cave walls in Tibet (Hevajra, Yama),
blue of fear & the far distance,

        walls
of the Lama's stable where scythian ponies
turn their flanks to the enquiring light:

the blue is dark, the blue is sight enough for us
who carry them   the strange   places that they go
with bells & shaky musics & we run.

FEBRUARY'S LAST SONG & DANCE

now when the heat
starts
    & the heart
heaps up its winter
to take
inside
    & be
everywhere
to itself its such
& such
    austerity,

come where it claims
to be outside
after acacia
& as the cactus even
flowers
    & my sense
goes away
this crazy day

everything only the
color of itself.

A ROMANTIC REVIVAL

*(Chausson's Concerto for Violin, Piano
and String Quartet, Op. 21)*

Pointed arch ∧ Ogive of the first

movement, a

rhythm   by which the man knows himself

             restored, restored by energy,
specifically,
        by what he calls *his,*
               his own.

         It is my own, he says.

It is my arch & it leads
through the wall long blind
newly to within
         a penetral dark   from which I heard   music come
so I knew the way

            *

Yet it would be melodic despite
all he could do to make it his own.

       Melody is no man's. 'Our song'

Chausson writes: "Not that my taste for nature is diminishing,
but I am seeking something other than the object itself."

I read on the record jacket: "this eternal swooning before one
tree, or two trees which form a bouquet, or three trees which form
the beginning of a forest, irritates . . ."

—something other than the object itself.
          Not the start of some woods,
not the borders   of a material world.

Unworld   where the structures of melody
outlive the song

          & there are no trees,
                    "except what I make up"
when I see that clear.
          Bloody sunday
          after the only war.

              *

So we woke to it, the cat writhing in a fit,
crashed around on the kitchen floor
under the window where
                    the rays of the full moon came straight in.
Came curved, heavy, wet
with too long regard,
            an eye
          that is all white

looks on the torture of the physical body, the body,
as if there were no other.

Grave, Chausson calls it, stone in a field & it's dark
when I read the word as stone
& all night the fields belong to themselves.

          There is nothing that is mine.

Or: Nature is not to possess. *Have* is no natural word.

Grave. Across the field even a Romantic expects
          a sun to rise.

             What is my own
            but what I laugh at,
without laughter there is no sure relation.

            *

Any building fervently planned
obsessively occupied
          becomes a church. Every door an arch.

Music is intuited   inside the form
inside the solid—presumably the rhythm

breaks through & we go in—
                    he goes in
                    to a place that is his own.

A spirited place (très animé)
where beyond the object itself
the penetrated space
becomes a shape
                    a man exhausts all sides of

& does not lose himself?

If I listen to him I will hear him.
I will possess nothing.
If I listen to music
will he be happy?
                    Will he focus?
                              The general Moon
                    will be
on everything.
                    Its light annihilates structures,
statics the rhythm out at last.
The form is the life of the thing.
                              It's quiet.
The cat sleeps again
& through the window nothing thank God but the ordinary night.

THE MILL

On the other side of because
there ground a Mill.

It was the Mill of Particulars because we
heard the word. "When the word comes down, in that respect like
the dew, what can we do but wear it?" And so the mill was grind-
ing, and we were wondering away, what grain it knew for its own.
"Rice?" we asked it, "wheat or sesame? Simple wheats or millets,
kaffir corn? Barley?" we wanted to know. From the mill door
came the miller, dusty with his consequences, his face knotted up
like the face of a man straining at stool. "Point your words with
care," he said. "I have been chosen by this apparatus to conduct
the discharge of its energy. I have no responsibility to you or your
imagined grains. This is the Mill, and I am the Miller of Particu-
lars. Any other name, borrowed from Fable or Analysis, you
choose to give me will be wrong, dead wrong. Why do you detain
me from my work?"

We had little hope of learning
more from this man
so we shifted our feet
as we had seen
our grandfathers do
in the old man foot dance called
Becoming the Grass.

"At least appoint a time," our headman cried
out, "when we can approach the Mill with what we have, to get
what we need." But the Miller declined to answer, and closed
himself again inside his Mill. But it wasnt his, we thought and
talked, it isnt his, it's ours, our own mill on our own ground,
worked by our waters. These conclusions were a comfort, so we
broke up and went to our own homes, confident that in time the
Mill would declare itself clearly, its work and purpose and choice
of grain. Meantime we'd grow what we always grew, to eat and
make beer from and feed our animals and save some to grow more.
And time would tell.

And if time never did,
who among us
would ever notice or recall

when that time began,
or stand out some day
before the mill
to call the Miller out
to answer for his bluff
and grind at last
whatever he thought
to bring with him?

EQUINOX 1972: THE SURFACES OF SPRING

It is something to sit in the sun
beautiful
   the folding chairs against the high blank
          highschool, wall,
reflecting on their faces,
        day of sun. Surficial sun. An hour
of it,
   Crown Street & Nostrand the old women would
take it
in
 (all my life, last seen '61,
        late winter)
          warming their old year.
I have seen them
in December
if the day lets.

       *

       The time
       is going on,
         to hear
       & try again.

    What I dreamt of was a pitch pipe
round like the one my mother brought home before I was born
      to set voice against
     in fair comparison,
         pitchpipe

    & the natural
instrument.

       *

Das Herz, der kleinste Bienenkorb, umgibt
die andern alle
     (2nd Bass solo in Webern's Kantate Nr. 2, Op. 29.
     Text: Hildegard Jone.)

The heart, that smallest beehive, surrounds
all the others.

        sacral   tonus
lissome healthy muscle is a hymn of 'sudden grace'

                        a row of miracles.

           *

Smallest insects in the chambers of a yellow rose
        no lips no heart for them
for them heart's no lips, no rose yellows, a face
      is enough for the calm of them
able to pass or to rest on those surfaces alone.

THE LEAVES

        "You've worn them long enough,
Orpheus,
        let them fall away, among the mottled leaf shadows
under the gay beechtrees
           that console us for sorrow
before sorrow—"

        There is a map
I'm reading it—location
        is enough for any passion.
The thing has no meaning but what you put in, Invention,
to make it is to find it there. Contradictions.
        trobar, & theory of.
Can be found only by being made. But it is found.
And what do you find in those tall green bottles
worth carrying across the sea?
        & if not ecstasy,
why cork it in, & what release
        if not release?
        A cloud
over some mountain—that's its job, to be there
& we endure the distances.
        And Strindberg
burnt the skin off his hands in Paris,
making gold—
        "my art
is enough to behave to," said Olson,
of whom Helen dreamt last night,

that he came back from the dead,
        that one does come back from the dead
& wondered if he'd be welcome
        to come again
to this neglected city of the personal.
        The only
accurate.
        Panpipes (streets),
        that one breath can be many voices,
        divided over the hollowness of things,
        the apertures,
        the silences.

"The Life
comes down & comes in.
It is an easterner
sometimes remembering East,

he wears a sweater
still stained with a not long ago snow
or the salt to melt it,
his old home."

A MEASURE

Some nights the moon straight overhead is not far
it is a node in the spine, a woman
could easily reach it combing her hair.

THREE TUNES (ONE FLAT) FOR A YOUNG POET

1

Capricious young man
the goat of whom
I much regarded:
           close the book
        if it unthees me . or turn
to face me your anger . straight
        not as a critic fares
wormwise through a blinded text.

2

And it isnt all Orpheus
or if it is, a face
we havent seen in the operas & paintings of
opens her mouth on the rostrum—
the Man gnawed to death by the Woman in him
tries to choose one of them for life & fails.
This failure (this adultery)
is the impersonality of art.

3

Too hot to be two handed?
A limber thumb
untunes the sun.
David rests in the shade.
He is a cutworm—
no leaf safe from his song.

THE ANTIQUARIAN

                    stood or sat or felt
the intricate accounts that led to him.

They ran from all parts of the Going On,

                    the 'forest'
he'd let it be called.

          These are his relationships,
these are relations,
                    the wrong or righter
times for doing things, rites, maps,
lexicons. Details to be committed to.
Drugs to engorge. Facts
          that made love to him
all across the street & under
the disused el station, streets
stripped, dust coming up, light
coming from somewhere,

                    the times of things
multiply inside him.   Truth
caresses him
          with her instances.
                    She is bare
of every quality
but connection.

TWO LOVE STORIES BETTER THAN AVERAGE

1

In the middle of it flying through the air
a certain sailor of intimate relations related
a red negotiation across the better part
of the little island with so many sheep.

2

A xerox of a hand inscribed *all over you*
was the love letter she woke up to find.
She shivered with foreknowledge, at a brutal
playfulness the letter wielded, the sun.

THE RETURN

Twisting the word around
to make it fit
the dusty corners of no man's house
as if it could
be the word of that house
never yet spoken in spruce or linden
or all the old nameless wood
lath & rafter.

SUMMERTIME
                    for L. Z.

Around the edges
                    or Red Asparagus,
        a galliard for an unlikely Friday

's special, fisherman's platter & O
        (pronounced ♀)
all the fish she can eat
                    "and makyth for a strong stink
later, in the Stall."

                    It's not so hot.
Blast of the trumpet
                    (truth,
            etymon, troth)
                        against infectious sleep
            who yet our brother is
                        & one like him
prevents the End.
                    This is the region of Moskito Byte
& little fly this
morning on the kitchen
table too
            early to kill.

WAITING FOR THE BARBARIANS

Who will they be
coming in
like a springtime
whereof we recall

mostly the bugs
but the flowers
blossomed & birds
adorned the day so

long it was night
before they left—
it is not a matter
of rabbits. Who

are they who come
longarmed, leaning
on the gunwales of
soviet tanks, spiders,

organizers, bathrooms,
coffee with roasted
barley, movies, wings,
translations?

NY 97

Road north into summer
childhood by river
white stone . "whiffletree"
        "corncrib"
& cabbage from cowshit,
                the old wagon,
        & his face dark brown, turned
        in shadow, from the sun,

the old man

                *

foot caught in buckboard
favor my ankle after

blueblack snake dead on the lawn

                *

naked at three on warm rock
lift my soft arm

a kingfisher goes down.

AITHERS

What does the sky remember
of those who came down to us
from crystals whose axes ran
through spaces closed to our eyes?
Between me & the stars can I
look out & find their traces?
The stars are under my feet,
my flesh is their only Remember.

And Space, where do you live
beyond the instructive vacancy
mirrored brilliant in our books?
Are you built of numbers
or are the numbers only your road,
footsteps left as you pass?

A PRAISE OF ORNAMENT

that the wall in ever
receding angles meets
an ever advancing eye

that we go to the world
& are gone in it
& the gold

intentions, lilies or lions,
stand up for ever
from the crimson ground

where we only
once shall have
travelled.

ORION'S CAVE

Open the middle of the tree
folded paths, the sheaf
of all grown meanings
pointing to the flat sky.

The traveller comes into Utah remembering trees.
He wont stand in their shade till the Sierras
if he gets that far.

                "Freyr Ingve inn Frodhi, Lord Ingve the Fertile, was carried from his fane at Uppsala, carried in a wagon. No one dared to look in. The priests led the cart, and his travel was understood by the land as receptivity, growth, fulfilment of form, rich harvest. His track."

Those are the lines of the machine.
What he eats,
how he gets that way.

Some see him as a hunter,
others, as the instrument itself
a net spread to trap birds.

Of course I see him as a lover,
his bright sword a phallos
shining but at rest

satisfied with the world as woman,
I mean after the act.
Mostly now he travels.

Or unravels our fertilities
so caught up in webs of
ownership & nets of
what are we going to do.
There is no blood on his hands.

  . . .

It was strange to see him in California, standing over the San Gabriels on clear winter nights, or to watch him ahead of us

when we drove home late, he on his side over the valley. On
his side. Paranibbana of the Buddha. The Mind Substance put to
sleep.

He "lay on his side,"
his right side—

        (that haunting poem of MacLeish, the woman,

but it was not a woman, it was Orion,
      called in this text Freyr of the Vanir,
        Lord Ingve, the God Frey.

He lay on his side & the mind slept.
All the poems that haunted it
were quiet. All the memories
of its own creation, husks & ogives
of its accomplishments, its
"magnificence," slept too.

The tree opens there
            there is nothing inside it
inside it but the idea
          idea of growing

growing wood.

Now that wont burn in our campfires.
No chill
      burnt off by that hyle.

Nothing inside it but the idea of growing.

Period. No wood. No hyle. No matter.
The fire burns in the mind & is the mind

& burns the mind—
         he called down to me
         as he lay on his side.

. . .

She saw a mouse or shrew

dart under a car parked at the bar

the Cross is hidden every night.
   It is what we never see,
                          Canopus, mouth
of the furthest river
                  "substance of things hoped for,

not seen"—
            latitude is understanding.

A knowing
that is space.

. . .

On a grass triangle, four boys make the frisbee go round their
corners. Parallelopiped. Japanese beetle on the window, dont
let them eat glass. Trapped wasp. No special woman, across
the sea. Particulars of a daytime,
                        that lucent dream that gobbles
two-thirds of our hours. Day Dream.
                           The boys are hidden by the
trees between. One of them is a girl, I see now, her shirt blows
open as she swoops down to catch the skimmer.

Orion. Orvendel. Flight report: The World.

He skims us. Us=us, planet of, oecumene.
He skims us as my father in a dry season
skimmed flat stones across the Delaware,
all the way across to where the water & the
shore could not contrive to meet
on the sun-bleached gravel of that river's bed.

Skims as.

Shine. Meantime the music starts
if I remember. Remember.

I lay beneath those sideways stars & heard:

            there is no soul in the body.

114

Look at it
rightways, align
your sleep with my waking
& wake,

body is in soul.
Move
in that fertility.

And a man is lovely
& behave to him
also, I thought.
Mother is the name of him,
I thought,
what the tree meant
by the illusion of its wood
I pick up day by day & work.

.   .   .

42° North Latitude & the skies
utterly clear.
I havent seen them in more than a year.
Haywain near horizon,
the Milky Way a gas of going, Watling Street,
highway, home.

Item: that the turn from Kidd's lane under
Cassiopeia onto 9G
is entering the Milky Way.

Item: that this place knows me again.

On the hill by Grancelli's mill Andromeda
is bound to Morgan's apple tree,

apple green, "sea-girt"

And Orion is the pasture
where the horse is quiet

where the fox hides in the hedge.

115

THE VAN EYCK WORKINGS

Arnolfini's Wedding

The World

ARNOLFINI'S WEDDING

for George & Susan Quasha
17 XII 72

What we see
is not likely to be adequate

her flower, for simple,
doesnt seem.

We see a window & infer a door,
or see a door in that bright

convex mirror, gutter
of all mysteries.

The mirror is mercury
& mercury a certain sort of rain.

*

I have a city where the rain
also falls in golden globes

confusible with oranges.
Her hard slippers

are not just anywhere—
you can tell from the light it's recently rained.

*

Two people
& two more are going out or coming in.

They are Franz Völker & Maria Müller,
Louis Zukofsky & Celia Thaew

or a friend of Don Genaro & a friend of that friend.
It is two angels whose wings

imply a spectrum, they color the space
peacock they depart into

whichever side of the door they decide that will be.
It is me & mine

like any idle witnesses
hanging around a wedding.

They come to the door
& die to come in. Hello,

never all the way in, Goodbye
but never be gone.

*

We are stuck with a couple
damned in a doorway.

That is: there are Arnolfini & his
pregnant wife, then their reflection

in that vortex our mirror, & past them
two more shades

coming in or going out.
They are important

because they define a door.
A good marriage

has a way out built in.
There must be a door.

*

Surely the dog hasnt
been here forever,

dogs have nothing to do with always
& the narrow window

shows an edge of that kind street
we all do live on—that's clear

& that's where the dog can do it
if ever it has to be done.

The street's business
is only to intersect.

*

John of the Oak was here:
these words, as letters,

hang in the air
over the mercurial eye

that maybe saw & always
answered as if it did.

The words pretend
to be painted on the wall.

John. Everything pretends
to be just the place where we find it.

We find it sighing, we kiss it
singing, we call it Real

& measure with our newfangled minds
the distance from that glistering Real

to those heavenly twins our eyes,
& call that *the world*. That is,

the place where John was
when he wrote or said, *John was here.*

*

Now John is somewhere different
& if we had any sense we'd get out

121

before this philosophic wedding
seeps down to the heart

& we find ourselves married to the fact of it,
married to all of us!

one flesh of world & no divorce!

*

Was here. Last prisoner
in this cell-like fact, most

recent escape
from human physiology.

Every place you are
I have been.

Find my traces
& look past my eyes

to find the noplace
I look out at you from,

you lovely laity, come
levant with this shy woman

out of this box.
But the bed answered:

sleep in me.

*

Little figures on the finials
of the chair beside the bed,

little gods, cuculatti, hooded with earth.
They make sure the sleepers

dream of shifting to new houses,
each house more expansive

till they move to earth.
I admire Arnolfini

for being willing to sleep in this bed.
I cannot stand those dreams

of vacant lofts & basements & turrets
& cities to which we are forced

by invisible circumstance to come home,
set up house

with the mouse & ant, wait the thief
who carries off the plate & leaves

a sack of fine-milled flour,
trace of his nature. The granary.

The track leads into dream
& never back.

*

Over the bed a pregnant pendulous drape
hides a pomander to scent their sleep.

It is wholesome & banishes dreams.
It is one of her mother's tricks,

wisdom & all her fruits studded with cloves,
tracts, garnets, nails of the Cross.

Arnolfini has tricks of his own,
Tibetan, Sicilian, the small room

he wills to be married in.
His eyes without lashes. The world outside.

*

And why was there only one
candle lit in the candelabrum?

When was there ever
more than one light. These people

have seen their gods, their gods
looked just like them.

Their gods were coming through a door
or leaving a door behind them

by which the room & all the hundreds
of people in it could finally go out.

They can go out when the candles do.
Even now only one candle is left.

*

His robe is sable, from his trade in Muscovy.
Green her dress, Byzantine, swells out

a big round story where her womb is.
The bed is red.

*

Beyond the window the wind may move.
His left hand (the left

hand of a man is passive, magnetic)
holds her right hand.

He receives her. The energy
that made her pregnant

now flows back to him.
When the child is born

Arnolfini with open lashless unsmiling eyes
will lick milk from her nipples.

* * *

(*Coda, for the music:*)
This is only the beginning.
At the premiere of Strauss's *Guntram*

Rudolf Steiner will sit in the stalls
thinking about Bruckner recently dead.

The opera will be revived with Völker & Müller
the year America entered the war

from which, after all the deaths & all
his deaths, Ezra Pound will

float in a gondola, Olga beside him,
Paul Blackburn will face them, take the picture.

Ezra & Olga look into the room. Poetry
is not piety. Painting is not music.

Steiner sat alone in the stalls
& when he died his followers wondered

exactly who on earth he'd been.
Now John & Paul & Ezra are all dead

& are free to watch a wedding. For them,
all such festivals

comprise a city.
John painted the city. He said

it was bright enough but they had no light
because the Lamb was their light

shone in from another
picture in his mind.

The Lamb said: Weddings
& Deaths are exacly alike.

Paul said,
You'll be surprised,

the room
is really a door.

*

Arnolfini & his wife
in the silence we call history

enter the vermilion order of the bed.
We do not see it disarranged.

We look away & see outside of town
a stream move under trees.

A deer
stands with front feet in the water,

drinking. At this signal,
Ezra snuffs the last

candle with his fingertips.
The room turns inside out.

THE WORLD

for Helen

The world

map he
painted all
clear
no mystery
in those
distant windows
no,
    step
up to them

eyes mine

Artist
hunched
half in his
desk

what other
word fits him
(Father father
that voice or
voices hungry
at my white
shoulders
eating me
down o
father)

hush!
submit
to world!
it's the only
I allow

& he cares!
the painter
crunched
to his loupe

to see
what goes
in every room

the detailed tail
of that animate
woman he bade me
follow
only to play
her front part
her face
all over the waters
Maria
wonder
in her down
eating eye

humble
before the fact
her lap

this woman's
all face
her lap
snaps up
idle energies
once I thought
were mine

Creature!
admirable new
bearing Maria
new Eve
I sand my eye
to irritate

quanta of vision
discernible as
flesh

on this Field of Flashing Lights

or idle

wild,
I address you tonight
because a painter
got it right
& an obscure componist
composed
a line that masters
my mood to follow,

idle wilderness
of my affections
prick up your
yarrow &
answer me!

gl
ib
talking
answer
knows none—
he brews

this
Monday o lady
more than any

moon,
ampersand,
what I thought
was a crystal
was a shell
saves me from hell

there is no
form not
organic no
mind not mine

epistemon
& red flower

I'd rather
address a while
thank then

hoist the song
my flagrag
fluttering pole

this red
you gave me
time to find
I made

myself!
Hark:
every poem
is the T,
terminus,
end of the world

X
perceive my mark
& Xt receive
my sowle

which when my Lord
perceiveth
he releaseth
me from the empery
of Time his babbling
nursemaid,
from varlet Space
his earthly Tutor
& throws
the door open

I am the shuttle
meeting all the stands
on the loom of my life

& in my left leg
above the knee
I set
this metaphor to rest

& resume
on the red & green

checkered squares
of the Field of Flashing Lights
culled by two traditions
here first named
& budgeted to two
countries
of western Eurasia
after an Athenian
interlude
whose youthful children
were buggered every one
by the helots of
Hacademy

alas I need
that I need to
record
such unsex
when it all
could have risen
better
(redder)

in Plato's
unrumpled bed.
Porphyry!
Plotinus!

this I heard:
that Dee
from Prague
inducted
two traditions—
one went
by way of Fludd
to Vaughan
& Swedenborg,

& one to Kepler
at the court
of that same Rudolf,
thence to Newton
one way &

131

Goethe another—

William Blake
inherited the first.

England:
see *through* Nature.
Deutschland:
see *with* it.
Coleridge
shorted
Albion's circuit
by fetching
aus Deutschland
the sense of
Nature as evidence,
thus positing
the sense
of sense,
Natural Theology,
from which phlogistic
God has not yet
recovered

& Blake said No!
a woman is to fuck!
to talk to!
love!
go through!
not draw from, not
copy!

Portrait
of the Artist:
Jan van Eyck
concealed revealed
behind the smallest window
of his largest painting
now lost.
It showed

the World
& everything in it

clear
as if you were there

every part
detailed
& in one city
his own
house, his
glazed window,
himself behind it
infinitely small
reading a book
open to this text:
    This is the World
    & I have seen it
    & seen
    less than I here
    portray
    in power
    of this craft

ALC IXH XAN

my eye runs back
in terror
of this ancient man
to see the land
laid out
complete
& intimate,

azimuth
to reckon
what? zenith
how high is up,
nadir
when I shall come
to the earth again

to be Beside Myself
in flocculent
reminiscence
I will mistake

for gloire,
I glory
in particulars

& no woman
speaks.

(Father!
says my unborn
child to me,
I am alone
on your strong back
I am gold
& yet you lose me,
I am tight
but you pry loose,
I am the occasion
of your intellect,
come die in me)

& no, say I, no
it is not so,
unbegotten, unbegetting,
—sofort die Musik
schweigt—
unbegotten
unbegetting
I raid the horizon
for such stores
as I allow myself
to need, I suck,

I suck!

it is hopeless,
my psyche's
grammar
betrays her book,
I want no grammar
& have such grammarye
as friends have lent me
marveling
at my beauty

& their goodness
to see it so

Albion!
your cup is a year
& in it pours
the annual wine
Death fermented
& from it rises
intertwined with
fangèd snakes

the intelligible Rose!
I mean the thing
with Albion
is he sleeps
all our sleeps

we wake
for him

To specify:
an Italian beggar
come barefoot
with her sack
into the arbor
where we sat
under some growing
thing drinking

> Without a word
> she showed us
> inside her bag
> that it was empty

> I poured out
> what wine I had
> & bought with it
> her emptiness

> now I carry that
> upon my back
> & leave her to sit

in the shade

shuddering
of the vine
in every wind
that turns it
round

(turn me
turn me
Father!)
shut your face
I have to answer
that spits in mine

across alveolum
from east to west
I perceive
the caresses
of his small tongue,
he tastes like sleep
I have slept him
so deep
in every mirror,
dipped him
in Kastalia
where it flowed
down past Windham
& was cold,
my sailor hat
to baptíze,
across the ropebridge
pussyfooted
over Brahmaputra,
he fell
I did not
follow, I walked
to a cabin we

lived in up the hill
3 miles, the beer
almost frozen every
August morning

in the shade of this
selfish earth
hog hog
but it poured
easy enough
by afternoon, 112°
one day

& I forgot the water.
I bought a ring
death's ivory
head considered
which to bite
of what I'd touch,
I touched niente
nunca y nada,
I rode away
from his teeth
& ached in mine,

now this youngling's
tongueling
tangles
with my intended
invented word

tells me
in the mirror
convex
to reject the world
in all diffusion,
concave to hold it
in one point
& swallow it,

no glass
is truer
than the dark

—now her thighs
terminate in globes
translucent
not unlike

bowls for fish,
these globes
communicate
in fact comprise
one inner ocean
on which she stands
veering now to
red & now to blue

& is in general
concerned to mingle
according to a formula
"The Fact That Things Do Not Exist In Truth As Such"
the water of her intelligence
with the wine of my praise
pressed out by her same thighs
so far from Lombardy.

she pronounces it carefully:
"transfiguration of your dwelling place into Buddha realm
transfiguration of your being into god-being
transfiguration of every possession into sacred vessels of worship
transfiguration of your actions into real actions
this is the first stage"

& I have leave to wander
winter
all the way,
the day
of my the
is a sad lost day
when anything so
definite as an
article
went south
among the illegibly
highflying
I guess they were birds

they flew so
high they
threw no
shadow

             the bridge
shook a little
under my feet
under my shadow
why not,
quick breeze
dismissed my doubt
I crossed
again
to the island
I had shunned
the day before,
left my hat
home this time

no hat
no black or red or gold
between me
& the Sun

I hurry
to spill the beans,
I forget her names
she stood
I moved
the bridge
was a permission
a movie
I had seen before,
moved
only by the
dark we sat in

shared
the dark candy
found
in each
other's throats

sweet
not-sweet
a thick darting
or slender

blurring of no
possible line
my skill at
geometry
could endure

no line
but to heaven

no plane
but infinite

or I found
this Milky Way
warm as a shared
body we live in
a candy, the train
flashed past
on the Track of Flashing Lights

red over green
to signify
a destination,
simultaneity
open & closed,

imposed
on my religious head
by the optical behavior
of steel rails
the catechism
said were straight
& parallel
leading to
the familiar Nameless
Woman
so oft solicited
in Brooklyn nights
by the paladins
of inconsequence
we learned how to be

from those same books!

so the tracks outside
led on to Queens
around the loop
at Cypress Hills
where the cemetery watched
where we were going
bottles under arm
to the elusive
New Year
hidden up her skirt
& that Eve
most certainly found,

left
would have taken me
to Arlington
Library, its balconies
floored with translucent
ancient syrian rough green
glass through which my eyes
flowed up to apprehend
female shapes above me

when the tracks alone
were my concern,
out the window
of the mensroom
onto the marquee,
from there to the heavy
reek of pine tar
so close to the
wheels
flared
sparks
of only golden
red
to convince my mind
this
was the image
of what was to become
& what it was to come,
a fire
speared in pitchdark

with a fiery lance,
blaze
spun off a blazing sightless wheel

from that perch I saw
the blazing sparks
fall into the street below

city
you have eaten me raw
swallowed me down
until there is nothing
of my heart
that is not town,
I am riddled with streets

that's all I know,
& got it wrong,
was not an island
just
the other
side of the stream

just the other

fat with the dust
of my getting there
hat or no hat
dribble of sweat
through dust,
this is my face
Ecce Homo
this is animal
crosses to you
bareback rider
skimmer
of pond algae
knower of sandbars
proud identifier
of birds from birdbooks
I set my broad
sixfingered foot
into your stream

I
evangelize
my way
your way

I cross
to this other
condition
I had
called that

now this
is wet,
a leech
behind my knee
my thigh
above the tight
rolled jeans
is splashed,
halfway across
I am not different
from any buck,
with luck
they'll miss
if with their
luck they fire

the lucks
cross out,
I'm lone
amid the waters:
the condition
recedes, I'm there,
land
my feet
know how
more or
less to articulate

& in an alternate cabin
beside a decayed
Studebaker
I find my love

engaged with her husband
in polishing off
bottles of Budweiser,
as I always knew
I would find her,
I pull her on my lap
& we admire
how fast she drinks
& how accurate
his fire,

not for that
came I to this mountain,
I turn
& cross the Field of Fleshy Lights again
to green
my red a while
& attire
all my guess
in furs of certainty,
then hide
my knowledges
in weeds of ignorance—

now from my heart
which is defined
as the point of intersection
of my arms
I invite to withdraw
the chessboard
I had fucked with before,
those alternate
nowheres

& my hand
is somewhere
& my arm
& I stand
in no river at last
but this current
I have the way
if no will to
turn off—

Father Father!
again he cries,
how can I still him
from the easy
kitchen where he plans
my return to this planet
to sign the will
that enfeoffs him
of everything he has
just by sitting down & saying
I'm

who
do you think you are?
no think
about it (father
father!
I hear
the breath of a bad man
howling in your throat
father you're a bad
man father you're a
man father bad an)
end to this parenthesis.

How could the lion turn his back on the deer
how could the deer not look at the swan
how could the swan avert his eyes from Eve
how could Eve look only at the fruit
    he held in his mortal hand while he
        looked only at her
            only at her in all this world
how could the rabbit look at his heel
how could the stars in their musical cycles not warn the birds
how could the birds fly over & not hear or care

far out at sea a dark moon is waning

Adam & Eve
not really alone
in Simon Marmion's
landscape,
the endless sea:

that
began
or was beginning
when my eyes
not yet
had rounded
to enclose

I see it all,
eye
in the center,
body eye
marked
by her Cross

♀

I smell
the wood of her
joining,

pine hy-
meneal
& good greet,
pine elongs
& jasmine
softens
life to blur
socket
of his cheek
whose name
we do not speak

pine tar &
Creosote
's the word I
lacked, juice
keeps poles up
strung uneaten,
lamp line &
telephone,
cable
to her loin:

EAT MY POLE MY
FLOWERING STAFF
FOR NONE BUT
YOU BRANCHES
INTERLOCK
THE RIPE SPRINGS

which when she reads
a darkness
fiercer than her own
meets its
teeth in her night

it's all
experience,

knowledge
is what's about
her spine,
leads up
in darting
self-inhibiting
zigzags to the
left
the way a
snake climbs
trees

her spine
a knowledge
I have known
& have the time
to make it mine

the only land
between the web
flanged wet
feet of a swan,
Egg Highway
leads there
across the Field of Flashing Lights
red & green &
a greenish tint

to the white of eggshell

(father! I am left
in warmth
of a place you were,
I break too easy)

shut!

& the egg
pours out
its astronomic sun
& encompassing moon
strung
together with
that meek chalaza

(father!)

(brain) (egg)
in a (cup)
(skull)

the moon surrounding the sun,
in pilgrimage
around the hot stone
jigging a little
on the left foot
to the well,

hot foot,
Zam-Zam
along my gums
I fetch this
aqua home

:when the spark is quenched
in the general night
& only the smell
of creosote is left
across the tortured air
when the train has passed
& the street down there

148

goes back to its
natural nighttime
liquorstore glow,
heavy I-beams
of the city's will

the image
quenched
in the eye!

a well
to unanswer
every nation

a well
outside

& there are cormorants
riding the easy ocean
who dunk for food

plenty
time
the night

is always young

    [The Cormorants At Point Lobos

    engage to steal
    unimagined fish

    under the wet skin
    we permit them
        I came down
       to check out
        the rumor there were seals
    but the shiny
    black beasts in the
    cove were birds
        & I shared with them
       that terrible
    hunger for the surfaces of things

no depth can answer no
                              more-meaningful thing
make up
for the loss of that little bright meaning
if that is lost]

I came to her skin
because it shone

river
it moved & sun
that it appeared
to stand still

still shine

the world
in 'orbicular form'
displayed,
"where you can
recognize
not only all the
places in every
region
but also tell
by measurement
the distances
between"

What I was given
is a spirit

I hear it
roaring over the idle
time of my
soul,

be gold,
come out & rat
the black
earth at
last

Egypt all
these centuries
against your
mind

swear
by mind
you'll mean

& be wet
with that
other philosophy

Jan
nested
in his box
of windows,
a city,
your unborn
child
draws that way,

a box
with eyes

now lie down
beside the wood
under its bridge
immense
all but the eyes
my
breath hold &
tarry

till he comes,
his footfall
my thunder

I do not answer
the flames
that are his ex-
clusive
conversation

except to be warm

except the world

& the glass
universe of Jan Van Eyck
painted to look like

marble enclosing
a wooden sky
painted like air
in which as an ocean
our behaviors
architect a space
full of
compromises,
temple
of inattentive will
swim
fondly
we
atlanteans
buried in air,

this
is Atlantis!

we are drowned
in will

our beams
of eyesight sore
from glare
of crucible
& spin
of wheel,

the potter
answers
when I will
& casts

a perfect circle

empty,
a girl lifts it
to her back
& bears it
all her life

negative space
for me to enclose

(confused, father?
lead it
on your back,
set it down
& make her rest

this glass
woman
you lust

in tricky
jungles
you invent
for her
to stumble in
hunting
your
lost mind)

(have you
children?)

(any!)

along
my road
that ran
from her

I refer
back to his text,
we have sunk
beneath a Nature
natured

by our un-nature
to suppose,

to suppose
it is empty,
empty,
Mantegna
will copy this image,

girl angel
with ball
on back

perfect gap
our vacuum

artifice of breath!

No space
too small

no twig
isolated
from his
tree's sight
so intricate

the mortal
senses
five
transcend
themselves

sight
by sight

special
function
(eye)
of skin
to see,
apprehend

see touch

The nucleus.

no space
too big

begins,
a sphere
"with corners
everywhere"

but a
wall
crumbles,
perfect garden
rosy brick,
apple drop
squirrel hunts
nuts
at dawn:

get there
before light
if you *really*
want to see

Now I take
my meetings
& my met

back to the net
woven before,
allow
my encounters
in this
sweet cloth

to rest

& eye contend
direct

with the Field of Flashing Lights
nowhere described
except in terms
borrowed from the eye
for lesser business
& higher
feeling up

over the horizon
each sense
implies

where the snapped
stick
knits
whole again

& no green no red
remain to be seen
only a circle
poured out of air

that he calls light
& drinks it down
my throat,
flashes like crazy
at the end of my arm

snow farm
where hydrogen
topples from the stars
& all my scars
feel
old again
when it touches them,

sea of matter
where the old battle
lurches on,
hulk against hulk

my one-armed soul
conquers

& falls
hungering
one last kiss!

then the swell
of natural rage
swims the ships
apart,

each vessel bobs
alone
sealed
in the sky bottle

in & out
& how
did whose fingers
work us in?

a book
throws off
its cover,
a red girl
of all your
myriads
peels

what leaves
I cherish
like a hard-won
high-school bra
tossed
from the car—

the Hay Wain
filled with the wounded revellers
of all our journey,

the leaves
go down
& the tree
perfects itself
at last,

revealed

& takes
what quiet
winter gives,
prodigy
of its immense
own nakedness

to stand
& gyre
on its sure
axis

pole of heaven,
its hands
are everywhere
while it stands
still.

The Field of Flashing Lights
he painted out
under the chair
of that young God Almighty
wearing the crown
of scarlet harlotry
while at His feet
unworn
the luminous crown
of natural order
vines its way down
into the sensible
universe
represented by the overpainting
Jan for unknown
reasons used
to hide the silverfoil
he used to hide
The Field of Flashing Lights

on which God's throne
had earlier reposed,
a sign & a promise

follow those lights
& snare
my image
at the breaking point
when your shortcircuited senses
dark out & the image
leaps & shatters

& all that's left is you

shattered in the center

Enlarge
this altar!

Let the woman's
will
become the world

& all illusions
lost
be found

in the russet brick
& bluish rock
towers of New
Jerusalem
painted
in the middle distance,
only a lawn or a
lamb away,
reached
through an act
of transsexual
worship
& no more marriages,

dome
of the Everywhere
Stone

he came to see

& left to be with
all day
everyday
& no forget.

From the bath
then
his women climb
steamy
purposeful
in the reek of herbs

their words
are soft,
the cat licks
water,
a lamp burns
what looks
like real light

a mirror
shows
their other side,
nothing's lost.

What is a witch?
a witch
is nakedness.

What is a world?
a vessel
"pierced, not broken"
by the light

no ordinary light
hereby made
ordinary

he said
& the mirror
answered.

All these vessels

are women,
all your women
those "pretty
cat-like"
women are vessels

the light
is not refracted!

the light is refracted,
the light
breaks,
the vessel does not break,

(Father!
have you consented
to the ordinary
light?
Father! have you forgotten
the delusive
paradise
between the flashes & the light,
have you forgotten
at last
the glint of flesh
you worshipped
for its own sake?
Father?
Now worship for mine!)

And I refuse,
the turban's folds
come half-undone
& lie
on my cold neck,
I have gone to Arabia,
I have worshipped
in the priestesses,
flesh & music
temple of the Blood of the Lamb,

I have come
from Arabia,

161

this light
is in my hands

a light
from nowhere

I have broken
over your houses

that the vessel
remain unbroken,

& the Field
of Flashing Lights

I have gathered
into ordered images

shaped by night
& colored by day

each object
in its intricate place

so you
can live in this world.

NOTES

In Mahler's Sleep. The title is from a poem of Gerrit Lansing, a phrase from "The Milk of the Stars from Her Paps," that spoke in my mind, starting the poem.

Then we came out & saw the moon is how my memory, the night in question, served up a phrase from the Sama Veda: a hymn to the moon, sung in Benares in 1951 by Rama Bhatta Ratate. It can be heard on Bärenreiter-Musicaphon disk BM 30 1 2006.

Eve of St Mark's. "On the eve of St. Mark, the ashes are riddled or sifted on the hearth. Should any of the family be destined to die within the year, the shoe will be impressed on the ashes." John Brand, *Observations on the Popular Antiquites of Great Britain*, London, 1853. I, 193.

A Red Figured Cup of the Onesimos Painter. To be seen on plate 19 of Bowie and Christenson, *Studies in Erotic Art*, New York, 1970.

Golden Gate. The reference is to chapter 50 of the Book of the Dead, which begins r n tmt aq r nmmat = the chapter of Do Not Go into the Rock. Page 108 in the Dover reprint of Wallis-Budge's interlinear translation of the Papyrus of Ani.

A Book of Building. American matchbook covers propose instruction. Helen found some she thought would provoke me, and so they did: blue-greyish badly drawn vistas of famous buildings, with a little letterpress on the back, telling about them. Big Ben. Arc de Triomphe. Eiffel Tower. Leaning Tower. Sphinx. There was a Taj Mahal too, but it came to nothing. I thought as I wrote from these things: all my life I've felt such trivial things, such degraded images, as obligations. Hence the theme of *all my life* crept in, ineluctably caught up with Bruce Baillie's movie to Ella's song. To amend these things. *Amende your selues*, writes Myles Coverdale, to translate Jesus's call to *metanoia*.

Waiting for the Barbarians. The title of course of one of Kavafis' best known poems.

Orion's Cave. A celebration of the sky and some of its perceptible beings—dependent on the splendid *Hamlet's Mill* of Giorgio de Santillana and Hertha von Dechend. Besides all the substantive and quizzical syntheses, the book also offers one of the rare public surfacings of the work of Leo Frobenius permitted in America.

The World. Through the poem emerge many images from a number of extant paintings of Jan Van Eyck. No need to identify them, since he caused the images to exist, and they do exist, so can enter the world freely like any other existing things.

Reference is also made (via Panofsky) to Bartolommeo Fazio's descriptions of some works of Van Eyck no longer known to be in existence, particularly a delighted account of a painting which showed naked ladies (witches, Panofsky

163

guesses) emerging from a steamy bath, where a painted mirror showed their painted other sides. More important is the description of a round painting of the whole world, which gives a title to the present poem. The Latin text can be found in Panofsky's *Early Netherlandish Painting*, I, 361, quoted from Fazio's *De Viribus Illustris*, and can be englished: "By him [Van Eyck] is a representation of the world, in orbicular form, which he painted for Philip, Prince of the Belgians, than which no more consummate work can be imagined in our age; in it you can not only see places, districts and regions, but even tell, by measuring, the distances between places."

ALC IXH XAN is usually taken simplistically as Jan's odd way of writing *als ich kann — as I can*. It is his motto.

R. K.

PHOTO: Charles Stein

Born 1935, Brooklyn. Since 1961 thirty or so books published, most poetry, few prose. Of these, *Armed Descent, Axon Dendron Tree, Finding the Measure, Songs I-XXX, The Common Shore, In Time,* and this present book, *The Mill of Particulars,* seem now most important to me. In Los Angeles, as Poet in Residence at Cal Tech for 1971-72, I composed the long poem called *The Loom.* These days I'm at work on a prose transformation, *Parsifal.* I teach at Bard College, and live with Helen in Annandale.